CW01455211

A
Story
For
Jessica

Dedicated To All Children
Who Have
Two
Houses.

My name is Jessica.

and

I have

TWO

Houses.

During the week, I live with my Mama.

I go to school...

ride my bike

swing

And sometimes I get to
go ice skating!

At my mama's house, I have a cat named Jack Cat.

...And
I have a big brother
who is a teenager.
His name is Justin.

I like living at my
mama's house.

On the weekends, I
live with my Daddy.

I play with my cousins

and ride my scooter

I play dress-up

And sometimes I get to
go ride go-carts!

At Daddy's house I have a new puppy.

...And I have two
little brothers
named Devin and
Cameron.

I like living at my
daddy's house.

Sometimes I feel
sad because I have
TWO houses.

Sometimes I miss my Daddy...

I MISS YOU

...and sometimes
I miss my Mama.

Sometimes I feel
happy because I
have TWO houses.

Santa Claus comes to BOTH my houses...

and the Easter Bunny brings me
TWO Easter baskets.

I wish we all lived in ONE house.

But since we don't...
I have
TWO
houses.

The
End

33989961R00018

Made in the USA
Middletown, DE
21 January 2019